The R-Future Workbook

The Companion to the Annual Conference for Regenerative Entrepreneurs
Your Step by Step Guide to Envisioning Your Best Life, Your Regenerative Business Plan, & More!!

Copyright © 2020 Matt Powers
All Rights Reserved
Written by Matt Powers
Cover by Matt Powers
Formatted by Matt Powers
Printed through IngramSpark

Send all Inquiries to:
Matt Powers
Matt@ThePermacultureStudent.com

Published and Distributed by
PowersPermaculture123
ISBN: 978-1-953005-02-1
website: www.RegenerativeSoilScience.com

Please Note: The information in this book is meant as an educational and informational resource and does not represent any agreement, guarantee, or promise by any party associated with the creation or editing of this book. The publisher, editors, and author are not responsible for any negative or unintended consequences from applying or misapplying any of the information in this book.

CONTENTS

[1] Introduction

[2] Day 1

[5] Day 2

[8] Day 3

[11] Day 4

[17] Day 5

[23] Final Thoughts

[24] Lined Paper for Notes & Extended Answers

INTRODUCTION

If you have ever asked yourself:

How do I do the right thing and still make a living?

Or

How do I improve the world we live in while living in it?

Or

How do I start a regenerative business?

You are in the right place. In this workbook, you will find the steps to make your regenerative business plan or to get inspired to start on the path, R-Future, the online conference, and this workbook are excellent places to start. This book is filled with questions that will guide your thinking and writing. It's designed to accompany the R-Future online conference experience. It will help you organize your thoughts, keep notes, and direct you towards your goals. There's a business plan guide. There's Convener's Questions from Alan Booker. There's a lot to consider when we start any sort of regenerative business, so writing it all out is vital for us to understand, communicate, and launch our ideas completely and successfully.

DAY 1: BRING THE ENTHUSIASM

Thursday Jan 14th

Conference begins – your journey is at its start. The question for today is: WHAT BRINGS YOUR ENTHUSIASM? Every day we are making choices and those choices affect our level of enthusiasm about our life and ourselves. Let's identify and write out what makes us enthusiastic and identify those things. If we can see what makes us feel more alive, we can figure out what we can do to best serve in this life, what activities we'll never tire of, and how we can make work an extended game of play that makes life better for everyone.

Day 1 WRITING ACTIVITY

- **What Brings You Enthusiasm?**
- **What Can You Do To Magnify That In Your Life?**
- **What Business Ideas, Services, or Roles Fit Your Enthusiasm?**

Use the following pages to write your answers to these questions, BUT don't feel restricted to this area – you can flip to the back and use lined pages back there as well. This is your book to fill it in as you like and hopefully this is just the seed of a lifetime of books you will fill with your ideas that eventually become reality. It all starts with putting pen to paper.

DAY 2: WHAT IS YOUR WHY?

Friday Jan 15th

What is your WHY? This is a key question for us all: it's the motivating reason behind our actions. It's different from what brings you enthusiasm. You just love those things, but there's a reason you want to accomplish your goals likely connected but sometimes separate from what brings you joy and energy. You may have faced challenges in your life that compel you to help others in similar circumstances. Helping people might be what makes you enthusiastic, and your why might be because someone did or did NOT help you. You may just get energy from talking to people and you find that you want to use this skill to talk to folks that really need it and it may be very hard for you and even dangerous depending on the circumstances, but you find that the energy you get from tapping into your enthusiasm powers you through the hard work. That's what I've found in my own life: we can create an engine of enthusiasm to power ourselves to accomplish great things if we know our specific enthusiasms and if we know our individual why.

Day 2 WRITING ACTIVITY

● **What is your WHY? What is motivating your goals?**

Use the following pages to write your answers to these questions. Remember you can flip to the back and use lined pages back there as well. Sometimes there's a WHY beneath the WHY…

DAY 3: HOW WILL IT HAPPEN?

Saturday Jan 16th

Every invention that ever was and is once was an idea in someone's head. The same goes for all the businesses too, so start envisioning a detailed map of your future. If you can see where you want to head, you can at least begin to map out a series of steps that must be accomplished or things that must be true for it to happen. We not only need an operational business plan, but we need a startup business plan to seed or fund the business to begin with. We can start small and regeneratively and scale up, but we need to know where we are and where we want to go first, then we can sketch out a path, and only then can we begin to verify, run the numbers, and get advice on our ideas.

Day 3 WRITING ACTIVITY

● What is your regenerative business plan?

- Mission Statement
- Structure & Systems of Operation
- Revenue Cycles Products & Services
- Audience
- 5 Steps Toward Success

DAY 4: WHAT WILL YOU OVERCOME?

Sunday Jan 17th

Today is about reflection and taking the time to think deeply about what we are doing. We will face obstacles and challenges – we will not be able to anticipate them all, but if we do not ponder and reflect on their possibility, we may miss their potential to knock us off course, and when we are flying high on our mission, a few degrees off course can be the difference between arriving at our destination and crashing into the white face of an unanticipated mountain once we have flown a few hours, and we want to go all the way. We in it for the long haul – we are all in it to regenerate our world, to set our economy and human systems onto an ethical and regenerative path. We know our WHY and HOW of our Regenerative Business Plan – now it's time to think about the HOW more deeply. What can go WRONG?

Day 4 WRITING ACTIVITY

- **What will you have to overcome to achieve your goals? How will you accomplish it? What do you need to learn?**
- **Write down any new ideas or revisions you might have to your business plan**
- **Answer the Convener's Questions (on the following page)**

THE CONVENER'S QUESTIONS

From the Integrated Regenerative Design framework and the Biocompatible Design Book by Alan Booker

1. Is it needed?

2. Is this the best way to meet that need?

3. Can it be done without harm?

4. Can it be done ethically?

5. Can the results be ecosystemic, biocompatible, regenerative, and profitable?

6. Will it support our desired quality of life?

7. Is this the best use of resources?

There's more lined pages at the end of the book if you run out of space (friendly reminder).

DAY 5: BUILD YOUR MOMENTUM

Monday Jan 18th

Now that we've put in the time, the reflection, and the analysis: let's put it all together and get it working as a holistic system. These are big picture questions that will inform and refine everything that you do from this point forward.

Day 5 WRITING ACTIVITY

- **How does everyone benefit from your business being successful? How can you communicate that?**
- **Who will you invite to join you and support you on your journey? How will you invite them? How will you retain them and still bring them value?**
- **How will your business become MORE REGENERATIVE over time?**
- **What are your benchmarks/metrics for regenerative success over time? And what is your timeline?**

- **What 5 things must be TRUE for your businesses goals to be accomplished?**
- **What would a Kickstarter or other crowdfunding campaign look like for your business or product?**

FINAL THOUGHTS & QUESTIONS

Thank you for being a regenerative entrepreneur – you are the key to a brighter future. Your choices and actions are influential beyond measure, and I'm so honored to to help you on your journey. I hope this conference, this workbook, and way you think and feel right now will stick with you and help propel you to your next level!!

Grow Abundantly, Learn Daily, & Live Regeneratively,

Matt Powers

FINAL WRITING ACTIVITY

- **What new insights did you gain through this process?**
- **Has this conference changed your life? If so, how?**
- **What are you going to do differently now?**

www.ingramcontent.com/pod-product-compliance
Lightning Source LLC
Chambersburg PA
CBHW081758100526
44592CB00015B/2478